THE COST OF RESILIENCE

How I Stopped Calling Pain Strength

Nia M. Thomas

The Cost of Resilience: How I Stopped Calling Pain Strength

© 2025 Nia M. Thomas

This book is a work of nonfiction. Names, characters, places, and incidents are drawn from the author's life. Some identifying details may have been changed to protect privacy.

Published by **Strong Roots Publishing**
Austin, TX

ISBN: 979-8-9934110-0-2

Book design: Strong Roots Publishing
Printed in the United States of America

For my mother, whose love and sacrifices have shaped me. Even through everything, your presence is felt on every page.

My father, my aunt, my uncle, and my sister, your lives molded me, and your losses shaped the fire in me. Even in your absence, you continue to teach me how to endure, to love, and to rise. You planted the seeds of resilience deep in my soul, and I am who I am because of you.

To my sister, your strength, love, and loyalty have carried me in ways I can never repay. After our father's passing, you stood by me and cared for my mother as if she were your own. Your presence in this chapter of my life has been a gift I will always treasure.

To my circle of girlfriends who have walked beside me through every silent battle, thank you for showing up, for listening, for laughing, for covering me, for holding space when I couldn't hold myself up, and for reminding me who I am when I forgot.

And most importantly, to my husband, your love, even from behind the wall, has carried me through storms I didn't think I could survive. You've grounded me, challenged me, and reminded me that even in isolation, I am never alone. You've been more than my spouse; you've been my lifeline.

"I am shaped by what tried to break me, but I am not defined by it."
— Nia M. Thomas

INTRODUCTION

This Wasn't Supposed to Be My Life

I was raised in love.

Two parents, both working, both present.

We weren't rich, but we were alright.

Family cookouts, Christmas mornings, and, house full of warmth and laughter., I didn't come from chaos.

I didn't expect to end up living in the middle of it. But life has a way of humbling you.

It started slowly, little things unraveling.

A breakup after 12 years. An aunt I loved like a second mother was diagnosed with cancer.

A car accident with an 18-wheeler that shook me to my core.

Weight gain, surgeries, depression, and a quiet ache I couldn't name.

Then everything started happening at once.

I moved to Texas for a fresh start.

Months later, my sister had an asthma attack and was never the same.

I stepped in to raise her granddaughter, a bright but deeply hurting four-year-old.

I started dating the man who would become my husband. And then, he was incarcerated.

The pandemic hit.

I moved back to Jersey.

My father passed.

My mother started to slip away mentally.

And I still had to show up every day, at work, for others, for life. People see me now and say I'm strong.

I smile and say, "thank you."

But the truth is, strength isn't something I chose.

It was what I had left.

This isn't a story of perfection.

This isn't a highlight reel.

This is a story about surviving the unthinkable, over and over again.

It's about what happens when you're the one everyone counts on, and you're breaking too.

It's about grief, resilience, love, loss, leadership, and learning how to keep going even when you want to stop.

It's about what it means to be a Black woman in a world that often expects you to be everything, for everyone, without cracking.

I cracked.

I cried.

But I also grew.

This book is part memoir, part mirror.

You'll read my story, but you'll also find pieces of your own.

You'll be invited to reflect, to process, to reclaim your strength on your own terms.

I wrote this for the woman who's always "strong,"

For the one who doesn't get to fall apart,

Who keeps going anyway.

You are not alone.

This is for you.

This is for us.

This is proof that we are still here, and still rising.

TABLE OF CONTENTS

CHAPTER 1

The Split

We started dating when I was twenty. At that age, I thought I knew love. I thought I knew who I was, too.

Family and friends were deeply rooted in my values, and he and I spent so much time around each other's people that our lives eventually fused. His sisters became my sisters. My cousins became his cousins. Holidays weren't "his family" or "my family", they were simply ours.

On paper, we looked solid. We were like best friends, we laughed, we shared inside jokes, we could finish each other's sentences. But there was always something missing. That spark you can't explain. That deep pull, that magnetic chemistry that makes you feel lit up inside. It was never fully there.

It was like trying to fit a block into a shape it didn't belong in.

I ignored it for years. I stayed through his infidelities because it was comfortable, because marriage and kids and

THE COST OF RESILENCE

growing old together were what we imagined, and because, truthfully, I didn't know anything else.

And because I wanted children. We wanted children, badly. But my body didn't cooperate. Month after month, disappointment stacked up like bricks between us. And still, I stayed.

The breaking point wasn't loud or dramatic.

It was quiet.

After the last infidelity, I tried to work through it like I had before. I thought, "*If I just try harder, if I just push through this, maybe we'll be okay.*"

But one day, it hit me like a light bulb turning on in a dark room, I wasn't even happy.

Not "a little unhappy." Not "struggling but hopeful." No. I was miserable. And I couldn't understand why I was staying.

Was comfort enough? Was friendship enough? Or was I staying because it was simply easier than leaving?

That question haunted me.

I looked around at the life we'd built and realized so much of it was tangled up in other people, mutual friends, blended families, shared traditions. Leaving him wasn't just leaving him. It felt like leaving everyone.

THE SPLIT

But I chose myself, For the first time, I chose me. It wasn't clean. It wasn't easy.

We kept living together for almost two years after the breakup, not out of romance or reconciliation, but because, in this world, it made sense financially. At least that's what I told myself.

In hindsight, I can see it for what it was, security.

I had never lived alone. Ever. From my parents' house, to a dorm room full of roommates, to shared apartments, to living with the man I thought I'd spend forever with, there was always someone there.

The idea of an empty apartment, of coming home to silence, terrified me.

But eventually, I moved out.

The Day I Left

By the time I decided to actually move, tensions were at a boiling point. Living together after the breakup had gotten ugly, fast. The arguments weren't behind closed doors anymore. They were loud, public, and embarrassing. Screaming matches in parking lots. Tense silences that cracked open into shouting in front of friends.

THE COST OF RESILENCE

And I think he knew this time was truly different.

We'd broken up before, but now he could feel I was emotionally gone. That scared him. He started acting out, and I started realizing I couldn't live like this another day.

So, I made a plan.

I picked a date, quietly found someone with a truck, and waited for the morning when he would leave for work.

The second he closed that door, I went into action.

My heart was pounding. I had maybe eight hours, maybe less. He worked close by, and the thought of him coming home for lunch and finding me mid-move sent waves of panic through me.

I grabbed boxes, trash bags, anything that could hold pieces of my life. Each trip down the stairs felt like a countdown.

"What if he came home?"

"What if he saw me halfway packed?"

"What if this turned into something ugly?"

Because we were both stubborn. We both hated to back down. And if he came home while my life was sitting in a half-empty living room, it could have gone bad, quickly.

Load after load, hour after hour, I raced the clock.

THE SPLIT

Finally, after a few hours and a few sweaty, frantic trips, my things were gone.

The apartment was half-empty.

I was gone.

I sat on the floor of my new place that night, exhausted, shaking, and crying. The weight of what I'd just done hit me.

It wasn't just physically hard. It was mentally brutal.

That day broke me a little. But it also freed me.

The first nights in my new space were brutal, the quiet felt like it was screaming at me.

I'd sit in my apartment, staring at walls that didn't hold our pictures, feeling like I'd been dropped into someone else's life. There were moments of doubt, so many moments.

"Did I make a mistake?"

"Was I too harsh? Too impatient?"

"But slowly, the fog lifted."

I started dating. I started laughing again. And, surprisingly, the resentment we both had in those first months after the split softened. Our friendship, the one that had been the strongest part of our relationship, began to rebuild itself. We moved on with our lives.

But here's the part I didn't see back then, that breakup was the beginning of a bigger love story.

THE COST OF RESILENCE

"Not the love story with him."

"The love story with myself."

Leaving that relationship stripped me down to my rawest parts. It forced me to face my fears, of being alone, of failing, of not being "enough" without a man by my side. And in doing that work, I unknowingly started preparing myself for the kind of love I didn't even know I deserved.

Because the truth is: if I had never walked away, I might never have been able to see my husband, really see him, when he came into my life.

That relationship taught me what love isn't, and that clarity became the lens for everything that came after.

It showed me that:

"Love isn't staying just because it's easy."

"Love isn't tolerating betrayal to avoid being alone."

"Love isn't friendship without connection."

But it also taught me what love is.

"It's trust."

"It's vulnerability.

"It's being able to lay down the armor I had been carrying for years and let someone hold the real me."

When my husband came into my life, I was ready for that, I didn't need him to "complete" me, I had learned to stand alone. But because I had learned to stand alone, I could also stand with him.

The split broke me, yes. But it broke me open, and that's how the love I have now found its way in.

Reflection Prompt

Think about a time you stayed in something, a relationship, a friendship, a job, just because it was comfortable.

- What were you afraid of losing?
- What did you gain when you finally chose yourself?

Nia M. Thomas
THE COST OF RESILENCE

THE SPLIT

Journal Prompt

Write a letter to the version of yourself who stayed too long. Tell her what you learned. Tell her what you wish she had known. Thank her for getting you to where you are today.

_____

_____

_____

_____

_____

_____

_____

_____

_____

_____

_____

_____

_____

CHAPTER 2

When the World Crashes

Life was good. I had great friends, a close family, and I was actively involved in the world around me. My relationship had just ended, but I wasn't broken over it, life would go on. I was busy, loved, and full of energy. But there was this aunt of mine who made everything brighter.

She was my dad's baby sister, the youngest of nine, and the life of the party. People often said how much we looked or acted alike. I loved all my family, but she was different. She was my person. My comfort. I looked up to her because she just loved life so much, and she loved her family even more. I spent so much time with her that if there were seven days in a week, I saw her at least five. She was the young, fun aunt who could still get you straight if you were out of line.

For the last year or so, I started noticing little changes in her. My sister and I would exchange looks when something felt off, like we both knew something wasn't right but couldn't put our finger on it. Life carried on like normal, until the day it didn't.

Nia M. Thomas
THE COST OF RESILENCE

One memory stick out: my aunt threw a party at her place, a second-floor apartment in North Jersey with three bedrooms. Small, but that didn't matter, she had the DJ set up in her son's room, and the whole house was packed. Friends, family, laughter, music. It felt like a club, except better, because it was hers. We danced, we ate, we drank, we laughed until our stomachs hurt. That was her. She created spaces where joy lived.

She was my safe haven. When I couldn't talk to my mom, I went to her. Honestly, I'd talk to all my aunts when I needed a sounding board, but she was special. (Don't tell the rest.)

And then came the secret that none of us were ready for.

We all gathered at the hospital, confused and shaken. Some of her siblings already knew, but for the majority of us, we were about to be hit with news that would rearrange our world: stage 4 pancreatic cancer.

I rode home in silence, numb. Just a year earlier, I had been hit by an eighteen-wheeler truck and survived. But this, this hit harder. Immediately, I buried myself in research. Let's get a second opinion. Let's find another doctor. Maybe we can fight this. Looking back, I think she already knew her

24

fate, but she went along with my determination because that's who she was. She knew it mattered to me.

I stopped working and committed myself to her. Driving her across state lines for overnight appointments once a week, preparing her meals, picking her up for anything she needed. I didn't think twice. I loved her too much. She had been everything for me, and now it was my turn. I just knew I could nurse her back to life. I couldn't accept another ending.

Within the year, she was gone.

I grew up in a big family. Funerals were a constant. In a two-year span, I went to nearly a dozen. But this was different. She wasn't just an aunt; she was my person. Losing her broke me in ways nothing else had.

This was when my faith was tested. I had prayed every day of my life. But now I couldn't understand how God could allow this. For years, I stopped praying.

On the outside, life moved on. Within months, I was back at work, going through the motions. But something inside of me had shifted. Depression crept in quietly, and before long, it swallowed me whole. I didn't recognize it at first. I just knew something was off. I cried in silence, pulled

THE COST OF RESILENCE

away from people, felt exhausted all the time. Nothing brought joy.

Eventually, I hit a wall so hard I couldn't get back up. Within a year of her passing, I went on a three-month leave from work. I couldn't function. Couldn't get out of bed some days. I was overwhelmed by darkness I didn't have words for.

That was my introduction to depression.

Depression is often called the "invisible illness." The world doesn't see it, your smile can cover it, your work can distract from it, but inside, it's like drowning in plain sight. Researchers describe it as "a persistent state of sadness and loss of interest that interferes with daily functioning." For me, it was heavier: it was waking up every day to a hole I couldn't climb out of, no matter how much I tried.

Therapy entered my life during that time. Hesitant at first, I learned to sit across from someone and finally name what I was feeling. Naming it didn't fix it, but it gave me something to hold onto.

Even now, as I write this, tears blur my eyes. It still hurts. Years of therapy have softened the wound, but it hasn't healed completely. Losing her was the beginning of a spiral, the first wound that carved out the hole I've had to fight my way out of ever since. It was also the beginning of me realizing I was stronger than I knew, even if strength looked like simply surviving.

Reflection Prompts

- Who in your life has been your "safe haven," the one person who made you feel seen?
- How do you cope when your faith is shaken by grief?
- In what ways has depression shown up in your own life, and how did you recognize it?
- What small steps have helped you (or could help you) move forward during seasons of loss?

Nia M. Thomas
THE COST OF RESILENCE

Journal Prompt

Write about a time when you felt abandoned by faith or hope. What did you need most in that season, and how can you offer that to yourself now?

_____

_____

_____

_____

_____

_____

_____

_____

_____

_____

_____

_____

_____

_____

_____

_____

CHAPTER 3

Healing My Body

I wasn't the smallest, but I wasn't the biggest either. As a child, I was a little chubby. As a teenager, I was full-figured with curves but not fat. I was always active, we walked everywhere. As a young adult, I joined gyms here and there. I wasn't the most committed, but it wasn't a problem then. I looked great, I was in good health, and I was enjoying life.

Then one snowy day changed everything.

I worked a little over an hour away, and though the forecast predicted snow, my work ethic told me to show up anyway. As the hours went by, the snow came harder, heavier. Surely, they'd let us go early, right? Finally, about an hour before my normal end time, the call came: we could leave.

I headed down Route 80, cautious, alert. I was a safe driver, always thinking steps ahead. I felt the car slide once, but I didn't panic. I remembered what I knew, corrected it, and regained control. Whew, that was close, I thought. As I moved toward the exit ramp, relief washed over me. Then, in my rearview mirror, I saw it.

Not a pickup. Not a dump truck. Not even a garbage truck. A full semi, a tractor-trailer, barreling straight toward me.

Before I could react, **BOOM!** The first hit slammed into me from the back. My car spun violently. Another hit, **BOOM!** The trailer struck again, sending me spinning a second time. When the car finally screeched to a stop, I was sideways in the road. My chest tightened. My heart raced. OMG, I'm still here. I survived.

But then I saw it. The front of the truck was coming directly for my driver's door. Yup, this is it, Lord. I closed my eyes and prayed. The world slowed, and then it was over.

I came to, disoriented but alive. Cuts, bruises, pain, but breathing. The truck driver ran to me. A dump truck driver stopped to help. They tried to move my car out of the road. The sound of sliding metal still echoed in my head. I begged them to stop. I couldn't feel that terror again. They found my phone, and I called my parents, panicked, crying. They didn't know where I was. Emergency lights flashed. Sirens screamed. Firefighters pried the door open.

HEALING MY BODY

By the grace of God, I was discharged that night. Alive. Just cuts and bruises. A miracle.

But pain became my shadow. A slipped disc left me barely able to walk one block without excruciating agony. I couldn't move the way I used to. Slowly, the weight crept on, piling up so fast I barely noticed. My friends and family didn't notice either, or at least they didn't say anything. But I knew. This wasn't me.

For years, I lived in discomfort, disconnected from my own body. Who is this? What is this? I'd look at photos and feel unrecognizable. One day, staring at a picture of myself, I said, "Oh hell no. Something has to change."

I researched. I tried the gym again, but the pain made it unbearable. Eventually, I decided on gastric sleeve surgery.

The first three months after surgery were hell. I remember thinking, "Why did I do this?" Even half a cheese stick would make me sick. I was miserable. But I kept walking. Every day. Every chance I got.

Once I was cleared, I hit the gym, and I found something I hadn't expected: love. The gym became my therapy. My release. My sanctuary. I sweated out grief, anger, disappointment, and the weight.

THE COST OF RESILENCE

Within five months, I was down 100 pounds. I took my health seriously. I was more active than I had ever been, doing two-a-days at the gym, finding ways to move my body every single day. For the first time in years, I felt like myself again.

This wasn't just about losing weight. It was about reclaiming my life.

A Word on Wellness

Wellness isn't just about the number on the scale; it's about reclaiming your body and your peace. For me, the gym became the place where I could turn pain into power. Movement became medicine. It didn't happen overnight. It didn't come without struggle. But with every step, I learned this truth:

> *Your body is not your enemy, it's your partner.*
> *When you care for it, it will carry you through storms*
> *you never thought you'd survive.*

And here's the thing: caring for your body doesn't have to start with massive changes. It starts with one meal, one walk, one choice at a time. Choosing water over soda. Choosing to cook instead of grabbing fast food. Choosing to move instead of sitting still. Every single choice stacks up.

Eating cleaner isn't about restriction, it's about freedom. Freedom from sluggishness. Freedom from inflammation. Freedom from constantly being at war with yourself. Whole foods fuel your body in ways processed foods never can. Fresh fruits, vegetables, lean proteins, and healthy fats don't just change your waistline, they change your energy, your mood, your clarity.

The gym gave me strength, but food gave me power. Once I realized that food could be medicine, that it could heal me instead of hurt me, I wanted to treat my body with respect.

Here's my message to you: your health is your wealth. Without it, everything else, money, success, relationships, feels heavier. But when you choose to move your body and eat to fuel it, you're investing in your future self.

So don't wait for the perfect time. Don't wait for a diagnosis or a scare. Start today. Take that walk. Pack that healthy lunch. Sign up for the class. Try again tomorrow if you slip today. Your body deserves it. You deserve it.

THE COST OF RESILENCE

Practical First Steps Toward Wellness

- **Hydrate first.** Start your day with water before coffee, tea, or soda.

- **Move daily.** Even 10–15 minutes of walking, stretching, or light weights makes a difference.

- **Protein + plants.** Build every meal around lean protein (chicken, fish, beans) and vegetables.

- **Plan smart.** Wash, chop, and prep fruits and vegetables so they're ready to grab.

- **Cut the sneaky sugar.** Replace sodas, juices, and candy with sparkling water, fruit, or tea.

- **Prioritize sleep.** Recovery and rest matter just as much as workouts.

- **Celebrate progress.** Focus on consistency, not perfection, every step counts.

Reflection Prompts

- How has your relationship with your body changed during different seasons of your life?
- Have you ever had a moment when you looked at yourself and said, *"Something has to change"*?
- What does wellness mean to you beyond weight or appearance?

HEALING MY BODY

- How can movement, walking, stretching, dancing, become a form of healing in your life?

CHAPTER 4

Starting Over in Texas

I thought moving to Texas would be a new start. An opportunity to reset. A chance to escape the weight that had been following me. New city, new start, new me, right? I told myself that distance would quiet the pain, that if I put enough miles between myself and my problems, maybe they would finally stay behind.

But depression doesn't respect geography.

I left therapy behind when I moved. The mediocre care I had received before never prepared me for this transition, relocating in the middle of an active depression. Looking back, it almost feels reckless. I was already fragile; already broken in ways I hadn't yet admitted to myself. But instead of facing my healing, I packed up and ran.

At first, there was excitement. New sights, new work, new opportunities. And there were good moments, my work family quickly became my lifeline. If it wasn't for them, I don't know how I would have made it through. They celebrated me, checked on me, and gave me the sense of belonging I desperately needed.

But outside of work, everything felt foreign. The quiet in Texas was loud. There were no childhood friends to call, no family dropping by unannounced, no familiar hangouts that felt like home. I was living in a new world, and most days it felt like I was living in it completely alone.

The loneliness was amplified when my body turned against me. In Texas, I was diagnosed with a neurological disease. The words feel heavy, and the pain was unrelenting. Nights when I lay in bed aching, tears soaking my pillow, wondering if this was my new forever. I had no one to sit beside me when the flare-ups came, no one to witness the shaking, the numbness, or the fatigue that consumed me. Pain became my companion. And silence became its echo.

Still, I pushed forward. After just nine months of living in Texas, I bought my first home, alone. Signing those papers, holding those keys, walking through the doors of something that was mine, it was a high point. For the first time in a while, I felt pride. Independence. Proof that even in the middle of depression, loneliness, and a diagnosis I was still processing, I could still build something. That house was my safe place, even if I sometimes felt like a stranger inside it.

STARTING OVER IN TEXAS

But every victory had its shadow. Depression crept into the everyday. Grocery shopping felt overwhelming. Even surrounded by my supportive work family, I often felt hollow inside. I smiled, laughed, and functioned, but at night I fell apart.

And yet, life has a way of surprising us, even in the darkest seasons. In Texas, I went on my first date with the man who would later become my husband. He flew out to visit, and we spent time together laughing, exploring, and simply enjoying each other. He loved Texas as much as I did. Looking back, it feels like God tucked that trip into my story on purpose, a glimpse of a future that would one day anchor me.

Then came the pandemic. The world shut down, and the isolation I already felt grew unbearable. Depression deepened. Anxiety surged. The thought of being so far from family during such an uncertain time was too much. No amount of video calls or coping mechanisms could replace the physical closeness of being home.

So I left Texas.

It hadn't given me the escape I was chasing, but it had given me lessons. It taught me that depression can't be outrun, it has to be faced. It showed me the brutal weight of isolation, but also the beauty of resilience. It gave me a house, proof of my independence. It gave me a diagnosis, which forced me to confront my health. And it gave me a glimpse of love that would one day transform my life.

Starting over in Texas was never really about starting over. It was about learning who I was in the silence, in the pain, and in the loneliness. And even in those nights when I thought I couldn't survive it, I did.

Reflection Prompts

- Have you ever tried starting over, only to realize your problems came with you?

- What does loneliness feel like, in your body and in your mind? How do you cope with it?

- Think of a time when you accomplished something major (such as buying a house) while still struggling inside. How do you honor both truths?

- How do you respond when your health forces you to slow down and truly pay attention?

CHAPTER 5

Family Isn't Always Fair

Family isn't always fair, and love doesn't always come with logic, My sister was nine years older than me. For most of my life, our relationship was rocky. We loved each other, but love doesn't erase the cracks, old disagreements, unspoken hurts, and the tension that sometimes comes with age gaps and different life choices. We weren't always on the same page.

But just before everything happened, we had started to find our way back to each other. It felt like we were finally repairing what had broken between us over the years. We would talk on the phone often, dreaming out loud about moving closer to each other, and building a future where our kids and grandkids would know the bond we were working to restore. For the first time in a long time, it felt like we had a fresh start as sisters.

And then, out of nowhere, it all shattered.

She was only 43 when an asthma attack struck. At first, it seemed like something she would push through, scary, but manageable, the way asthma attacks had always been. But this time, it didn't stop. The lack of oxygen triggered a stroke, and within hours, the words no family ever wants to hear were spoken: "brain dead."

The cruelest part was that it happened while we were all visiting my parents, her, her two grandchildren, and me. One moment we were in the middle of a normal family visit, and the next we were in the middle of chaos, racing against time but losing.

By default, in those first weeks, her grandchildren stayed with my parents. They were already there when it happened, and none of us had the clarity or capacity to think beyond the immediate. My parents were elderly, grieving the loss of their daughter in all but body, and suddenly they had two children depending on them full-time.

I wanted so badly to take them both. My heart screamed for it. But reality whispered the truth, I didn't have the resources. I couldn't afford to raise two children on my own.

So, I made the impossible choice: I took the older one, and the youngest stayed with my parents. That decision gutted me. I still hate it. But it was all I could manage at the time.

44

FAMILY ISN'T ALWAYS FAIR

Even after bringing her home, I never stopped showing up for him, too. I sent money, made calls, and did everything I could to make sure he felt cared for. My family pitched in where they could, and I'll always be grateful for that. But nothing could erase the ache of splitting them.

Her kids needed stability, love, and structure. The eldest was already an adult, working to piece her life back together. But those grandchildren needed more than anyone could give alone. So, I stepped into the role of a second mother. Not to replace their mom, because no one could, but to hold space while the world around them felt uncertain.

One of my other sisters, the one who still shows up, moved to Texas with her family for a few months. She was my rock in that season. Babysitting, doing hair, and helping me carry the load. Even now, when I look back, I tear up thinking about how she showed up, not just for the kids, but for me.

And while I was carrying all of that, I was also grieving in a quieter, more complicated way. I wasn't just grieving my sister's health. I was grieving the future we had just started to rebuild. The phone calls about moving closer, the tentative plans, the small steps toward repairing what had been broken, all of it was stolen in an instant. It was like losing her twice:

once to the stroke, and once to the hope that she and I might finally find our way back to each other.

There were so many emotions tangled in those days. Guilt for not doing more. Fear that I wasn't enough. Pride that I had stepped up at all. I was parenting, healing, working, and unraveling all at the same time. No matter how much I gave, I still worried it would never be enough.

But here's what I've learned: sometimes being enough just means showing up. Even if you don't have it all. Even if you're scared. Even if you can only take one child at a time.

That chapter taught me that love often looks like sacrifice, and it's okay if that sacrifice comes with heartbreak.

And maybe that was the beginning of my understanding of resilience: not the shiny version people like to compliment, but the raw version, the kind that costs you something, the kind that reshapes you even while you're grieving. Later, I'd come to see just how much that cost really was.

Reflection Prompts

- Where are you carrying guilt for not being able to do everything?

FAMILY ISN'T ALWAYS FAIR

- What does "showing up" look like for you when your resources, time, money, or energy, are limited?

- Who has stepped in to share the load with you in hard seasons, and how did their presence change the weight you carried?

- How do you remind yourself that sacrifice doesn't have to mean failure, that love can mean doing the best you can with what you have?

Nia M. Thomas
THE COST OF RESILENCE

Journal Prompts

Write a short note to yourself releasing the shame of an impossible choice. Remind yourself that love is not measured by perfection, but by presence.

_____
_____
_____
_____
_____
_____
_____
_____
_____
_____
_____
_____
_____
_____
_____
_____
_____

Nia M. Thomas
THE COST OF RESILENCE

CHAPTER 6

The Cost of Loving Through Bars

When people talk about love, they rarely mean this kind of love, The kind where your partner is behind bars, and you're out here trying to keep life together.

The kind where every call matters more than most conversations in the free world.

The kind where your mail becomes a lifeline, and you rehearse your words before every visit, not because you want to sound perfect, but because you don't want to waste one second.

By the time he was incarcerated, my life had already turned upside down. But before the bars, before the prison gates and processing lines, there was just us.

We met at a wedding that looked like something straight out of a magazine. He was the best man. I was the maid of honor. We'd actually spoken on the phone about two months before the wedding, mostly small talk, but enough for me to think *he seemed interesting*. We even joked about

THE COST OF RESILENCE

linking up in Jamaica for the wedding festivities, but things didn't quite unfold that way.

At the wedding, there was light flirting, smiles that lingered a little longer than they should have, but no whirlwind, no rom-com kiss in the rain. It was subtler than that. Most of our connection started after we were back stateside. He traveled to see me in Texas, and that's when the spark turned into a flame.

We built everything on friendship. That was the foundation for something deeper. Something that could withstand storms *neither of us had seen coming.* He was ambitious, and I loved that about him. We would sit and dream together, talk about businesses we'd start, places we'd travel, the kind of life we wanted to build. It felt easy. It felt safe. And then prison changed everything.

People have opinions about women who love men in prison. Some think it's desperation. Others think it's weakness. But the truth? It's strength. It's connection. It's choosing to love someone for their soul when their presence is out of reach. And it's not easy.

Some nights I cried myself to sleep, not just for me, but for him. I cried for the sound of his laugh, for the safety in his voice, for the way he knew how to check on me without asking too many questions. I cried for the world that labeled him by a number, a mistake, a moment, while ignoring the man I knew, the one who'd stood beside me through heartbreak and hell.

Loving someone in prison forces you to grow in ways you never imagined. I had to become both *soft and unyielding* at the same time.

The Visits

Prison visits were their own world, one I wouldn't wish on anyone, but one I learned to navigate. Every single trip felt like a gamble.

The night before, I'd lay out my clothes like a schoolkid, only the "rules" for what was acceptable seemed to shift every time. Are these jeans too tight?

Will this bra set off the metal detector?

Will the CO on duty decide my shirt is too low today when it was fine last time?

I couldn't wear a wired bra, so I stuffed myself into a sports bra that barely fit. It felt like a punishment just to hug the man I loved.

Travel was its own grind. On Friday, I'd fly or drive into North Carolina, crash at my best friend's house about two hours away, and we'd squeeze in a little quality time before I passed out, because Saturday mornings came early.

Visitation started at 9 a.m., processing at 8. I needed to be on the road by 6 a.m. sharp.

I'd pray on the drive. Every. Single. Time.

Pray I'd be allowed in. Pray the visit wouldn't be canceled. Pray the vending machines would actually work so we could share a sandwich or some chips, because breaking bread, even with processed food, felt like a slice of normal.

And still, no matter how much I prayed, there were visits that got canceled after all the travel, after all the money spent, after all the hope. It was devastating.

The Emotional Toll

The visits were exhausting. I'd spend time planning, saving, and preparing for this one window of time. Then I'd travel for hours, go through security, wait in that cold, sterile room, and then watch him walk in with that big smile that made my heart stop.

All my annoyance, about delays, the COs, the vending machine, would fade the second I saw him.

THE COST OF LOVING THROUGH BARS

Every time, I wanted to run to him, to jump into his arms like some scene from a movie. But you don't do that in a prison visiting room.

Instead, we'd smile, hug, kiss, and sit down to savor every minute.

But the clock was always ticking.

Fifteen-minute phone calls, a handful of hours during a visit, it meant our entire relationship existed in these compressed windows.

Sometimes we laughed the whole visit. Sometimes we'd sit in silence. Sometimes we argued, and I'd leave feeling more broken than when I arrived.

There was one day, one I'll never forget, when an argument spiraled.

It wasn't about us exactly, but about something that triggered old wounds. I did what I'd always done when things got too heavy: I shut down. I started sliding my ring off my finger, half-thinking, maybe I can't do this for the rest of my life. Maybe I should just cut my losses now.

The look on his face, hurt, anger, disbelief, stopped me.

That one moment changed everything.

He was hurt, and angry. How dare I take off the ring? How dare I threaten to give it all up in the middle of the visiting room?

By the time the visit ended, we weren't laughing. We were still exchanging words, not in joy, but in pain and disappointment.

I left that day feeling defeated and angry. Thinking back now, I hate that we wasted precious face-to-face time on a fight. But life doesn't pause for visiting hours.

That moment taught us something, though.

It taught us to communicate better, to work through things instead of letting them sit like stones between us.

We both realized if our love was going to survive this, we had to get better at talking. We had to be open, raw, vulnerable, even when it felt impossible.

Learning to Communicate Through Bars

Loving someone in prison forces you to learn communication in a whole new way.

When you only get 15-minute calls, you don't have the luxury of dragging out arguments for days. When visits are measured by the clock, you can't afford to storm off and say, "I'll come back later." There is no later.

THE COST OF LOVING THROUGH BARS

We had to learn how to deal with the tension, the misunderstandings, and the pain. Right there, in real time.

And slowly, we did. I learned how to let myself be vulnerable, even when I wanted to push away. He learned how to meet me there.

We found a rhythm. It wasn't perfect, but it was ours.

Prison didn't just test our love. It reshaped it.

It broke me down. Made me cry in cars. Made me curse security gates and vending machine cards.

But it also made us honest. It made us grow.

It taught me that love isn't just about good days. It's about the ugly, inconvenient, heartbreaking ones too. And that's the love we have.

The Goodbyes

The goodbyes were worse than the hell of getting there.

After the hugs, the vending machine meals, the too-short conversations, after I'd finally felt him close, it was time to leave.

There's a certain weight to those last few minutes. I'd smile, force jokes, talk about mundane things like the weather, because neither of us wanted to say what we were really feeling, *I didn't want this to end.*

THE COST OF RESILENCE

When the CO called time, I'd hold him just a second longer than they liked, feeling his arms tighten around me as if we could make that moment stretch. But rules are rules. The guard's voice would cut through: "Let's go."

I'd turn to leave, my back to him, and that's when the real fight started, the fight to hold it together. I'd walk out steady, shoulders straight, because I didn't want him to see me break.

Once I cleared those heavy doors, the tears would come quietly, not sobs, just a slow stream as I walked to the car. On the drive back, I'd replay our conversations, every laugh, every hard work, every promise.

It was hard. It always was. But I'd push through, because that's what the road back home demanded.

SELF-HELP: Redefining What Love Looks Like

Growing up, many of us were fed a love story built on checklists and surface standards:

- Married by 30
- Two incomes, two kids, and matching pajama pictures for Christmas

THE COST OF LOVING THROUGH BARS

- Date nights, flowers, no baggage

But real love?

It shows up in hospital rooms.

In letters read over prison phones.

In therapy sessions and hard conversations.

In silence when there's nothing left to say, but the person stays anyway.

Sometimes, love doesn't come the way we imagined. But that doesn't make it less sacred. It makes it human.

REFLECTION PROMPT

- What relationships in your life have taught you the most about communication?
- When tension hits, how do you typically respond, by retreating, lashing out, or staying in it?
- What could change if you stayed vulnerable, even during conflict?

JOURNAL PROMPT

Write about a moment when love, or friendship, forced you
to grow. What did that moment teach you about yourself?

_____
_____
_____
_____
_____
_____
_____
_____
_____
_____
_____
_____
_____
_____
_____
_____

Nia M. Thomas
THE COST OF RESILENCE

CHAPTER 7

Leading While Breaking

Being a woman in corporate America comes with its own battles. Add being a Black woman to the equation, and those battles often feel doubled, sometimes tripled. I've learned to perform at a level that leaves little room for doubt, I can't just be good; I have to be exceptional. And truthfully, I am.

I've built a track record that speaks for itself. I've developed leaders, with at least nine people promoted under my guidance. I mentor other leaders who now coach teams of their own. I don't just do my job; I create greater impact. And yet, despite all of that, the struggle to be seen and fully developed remains.

The Invisible Ceiling

In meetings, I sometimes feel the weight of eyes on me, waiting to see if I'll be "too direct," "too passionate," or "too much." White male leaders around me can raise their voices, show frustration, even be dismissive, and it's accepted as "leadership." But when it's me, I risk the label of "aggressive" or "difficult." I've had to adapt, modifying tone, vocabulary, even posture so I won't be misunderstood.

It's exhausting. Leading while Black often feels like performing on a stage with no intermission.

Struggles with Leadership Development

One of the deepest frustrations has been my relationship with my own manager. While I pour myself into developing others, I often feel that same energy is not reciprocated toward me. I've asked for feedback, for coaching, for direction.

When I started to let my guard down and get vulnerable, I hoped for support and balanced guidance. Instead, the feedback came back harsher than I had ever expected. No mention of what I was doing right, no recognition of the leaders I had developed or the wins I had achieved, just repeated jabs at small issues I had already faced and overcome. It felt like my growth was being ignored, my strengths erased.

Meanwhile, I watched peers being pulled into rooms I knew I should have been in, conversations where my name should have been included. I heard my manager openly advocate for others, pushing them forward for opportunities. But when I expressed interest in going out for a position, that same support wasn't extended to me. I knew I was just as qualified, if not more, but the backing never came.

The company itself is great. I don't want to leave. But the struggle to find my voice in the middle of these dynamics is real.

And then there's the added layer of perception. Some leaders and team members assumed I wasn't engaged simply because I didn't present as the bubbly, overly cheerful "rah-rah cheerleader" type they were used to from others, usually white counterparts. My style is different. Steady. Grounded. Intentional. But instead of valuing that difference, it was too often misinterpreted as disengagement.

For example, I remember when my team's Gallup engagement scores came back stronger than ever. My team was thriving under my leadership, giving feedback that showed real connection, growth, and development. But in the larger group conversation, my results weren't celebrated. They were brushed past, overshadowed by leaders whose delivery was more upbeat and "performative." Even though my impact was clear in the numbers, the recognition didn't come. It hurt to know results could be overlooked simply because I didn't wrap them in the cheerleader tone others were comfortable with.

The Mentor Search

For a long time, I tried to navigate this alone. I thought maybe if I just worked harder, my results would speak loud enough. But results only go so far in corporate America. Access, sponsorship, and mentorship matter.

I started searching for a mentor, and not every attempt was successful. I talked to two different leaders, both of them well-meaning, but neither quite fit. One gave me generic advice that felt rehearsed, the kind you could find in any leadership book. The other wasn't invested enough; our conversations never went deeper than surface-level check-ins.

But then I found the right one. Someone who listened to me, who didn't try to mold me into a carbon copy of themself, but instead helped me sharpen my own leadership voice. Someone who challenged me but also validated my experiences, especially the parts tied to race and gender. For the first time, I felt hope that maybe I didn't have to figure it all out alone.

LEADING WHILE BREAKING (LEADERSHIP IN CORPORATE AMERICA)

Carrying the Weight

Still, the struggle continues. I've had moments where I've felt overlooked by leaders in my group, where my ideas were echoed by someone else and suddenly gained recognition. I've been left out of circles where key decisions were being shaped. And I've had to fight the quiet battle of proving, again and again, that I belong.

Leading while Black means carrying two jobs: the job you're paid to do and the invisible labor of navigating stereotypes, bias, and unspoken rules. It's fighting to show up fully as yourself while constantly managing how others might perceive you. It's loving the work but often feeling the work doesn't fully love you back.

And yet, here I am. Still leading. Still mentoring. Still growing. Still hoping. Because I know that every leader I develop, every voice I amplify, every barrier I break, it's not just for me. It's for those who will come after me.

A Word to Black Women in Leadership

To every Black woman navigating corporate hallways that weren't built with us in mind: I see you. I know what it feels like to pour out twice as much energy for half the recognition.

THE COST OF RESILENCE

To question your voice, your style, your very presence because others misinterpret it. To sit in meetings where your brilliance is minimized until someone else echoes it, but hear me: you are not the problem.

Your steady leadership is not disengagement. Your strength is not aggression. Your truth is not "too much." You don't need to twist yourself into a cheerleader to prove your worth. The fact that you're still standing, still leading, still pushing through glass ceilings that try to cut you on the way up, that's power.

We may not always be celebrated, but we will always be necessary. Our perspective, our resilience, our voices, these are the things that change organizations from the inside out.

So, keep showing up. Keep mentoring. Keep building leaders who will carry forward what you've started. Because your legacy isn't just about the role you hold, it's about the people you lift along the way.

Affirmations for Black Women Leaders
- My leadership speaks volumes, even when others don't acknowledge it.
- I am not "too much", I am exactly enough.

LEADING WHILE BREAKING (LEADERSHIP IN CORPORATE AMERICA)

- My presence in the room is power, not a problem.
- I don't have to shrink my voice to make others comfortable.
- The leaders I develop are proof of my impact.
- My perspective is necessary, valuable, and transformative.
- I deserve to be in every room where decisions are made.
- I am not here by accident; I earned my place.
- My style of leadership is not disengagement, it is strength.
- I carry the torch for those coming behind me, and I will not let it dim.

Reflection Prompts

- How has your identity, whether race, gender, or both, shaped the way you're perceived as a leader?
- Think of a time when you weren't developed or supported the way you needed to be. How did you respond?
- What qualities matter most in a mentor for you? Have you found such a mentor yet?

THE COST OF RESILENCE

- How do you balance being yourself with the pressure to "code-switch" at work?

- What invisible work do you carry daily in your workplace that others may not recognize?

CHAPTER 8

The Man Upstairs

He wasn't just my uncle. He was the man upstairs, literally, because he lived above us, and figuratively, because he always stood tall in my life.

Where my father was lighthearted, full of jokes, cookouts, and games, my uncle was commanding and direct. His voice could fill a room before he even walked in. When he spoke, people listened. Not because he demanded respect, but because he earned it. His words cut through the noise, sharp, honest, sometimes blunt, but always real.

To me, he was more than an uncle. He was like a second father. He pushed me when I needed pushing. He told me the truth even when it stung. He didn't sugarcoat, didn't water down his words to make them easier to swallow. And in that, I always knew where I stood with him. There was comfort in his clarity.

But my favorite memories of him weren't about his booming voice. They were about his strength. As a little girl, when I didn't feel like walking, he'd scoop me up and throw me onto his shoulders. Up there, I felt taller than the world. Safer than anywhere else. His shoulders weren't just a ride; they were proof that he would carry me when I didn't think I could carry myself. And looking back now, that's exactly what he did. He carried me through more than sidewalks and stairways. He carried me through life.

When he passed away, it felt like the ground shifted under me. Losing him wasn't just losing an uncle, it was losing one of my anchors. April 29 became a date I dreaded every year, a reminder of the hole he left behind.

I didn't know then that two years later, April 29 would take even more from me, that the same day I already mourned would become the heaviest day of my life.

Reflection Prompts

- Who in your life has carried you, literally or figuratively, when you felt you couldn't carry yourself?

- How do you honor the presence of people who shaped you with truth, even when their delivery wasn't always gentle?

THE MAN UPSTAIRS

- What anchors in your life, whether people, memories, or routines, help keep you steady when everything else feels uncertain?
- How has losing someone who was both family and a mentor changed your sense of self?

CHAPTER 9

The Day Everything Shattered

The call came just after I walked through the door. A friend from back home. Not a video call on Instagram like usual, just a plain phone call. That tiny difference made my stomach tighten.

"Are you home or in Jersey?" she asked. "In Texas."

Her voice shifted with urgency. "There are police cars and ambulances outside your family's house." She promised to throw on clothes and rush down the street to see what was going on.

Minutes later, she called back.

"They're not letting anyone in. Your sister's almost there. Hold on, let me find an officer for you."

I told the officer I was the daughter of someone inside, though I didn't know who they were there for. I hadn't thought it could be my aunt who lived upstairs, that thought never crossed my mind.

He told me my mother had been folding clothes in the living room while my father was in the bathroom. Then she heard a thump. I barely heard the rest until he said, "They're working on him now, and when they're working, we give them space." I knew what that meant.

I stayed on the phone while my sister arrived at the house. I put her on speaker as I jumped in the shower, hoping that moving through the motions would steady me. A few minutes passed in silence. "Prepare yourself," I told her. "It's been too long. I don't think this is ending well."

Another call came through, my cousin. I answered, already bracing for the words.

"I'm so sorry, honey. They said there's nothing else they can do."

My father was gone. The first man I ever loved had left me.

That night, I booked the first flight home. But when I arrived, grieving wasn't an option. My mother wasn't herself, and instead of falling apart, I went into caretaker mode. There were funeral arrangements to make, calls to return, and family members to steady. I was the strong one, the one who didn't have room to break.

It wasn't lost on me that this day, April 29, carried another loss. Two years earlier, on this same date, my uncle, who lived upstairs, who had been like a second father to me, had also passed away. That anniversary had already been heavy each year. Now, it carried twice the weight.

But my father's story in my life isn't just the day he left.

He was laughter and light, with a way of making ordinary days feel like occasions. He was the driver of summer road trips to North Carolina, the windows rolled down so the humid air enveloped us, the radio turned up just loud enough to compete with our laughter. A cooler in the backseat held sandwiches wrapped in foil, and the smell of barbecue chips and fruit punch filled the car.

He was the man who'd let me bury him in the warm sand at the lake, pretending to be trapped while both of us laughed so hard we could barely breathe. The sun would glint off the water, kids' voices carrying over the sound of splashes, and there he'd be, my dad, my co-conspirator, my safe place.

He had a quick wit that could make a whole room laugh and a quiet presence that made you feel safe without him saying a word. My humor came from him, sharp, playful, a little outrageous. We spoke the same comedic language, and he understood my jokes before I even finished them.

Nia M. Thomas
THE COST OF RESILENCE

He loved the smell of a good cookout, ribs sizzling on the grill, sweet smoke curling into the air, old-school R&B and house music spilling from a speaker in the corner. He thrived in the middle of a crowd, moving from one conversation to the next, checking on the grill with a drink in hand, making sure everyone had eaten. He was in his element when the house was full of family, kids running through the yard, plates stacked high, stories flowing, laughter bouncing off the walls.

He was an athlete at heart. Basketball was his game, the rhythmic bounce of the ball, the squeak of sneakers against the pavement, the friendly trash talk that ended in a laugh. Whether it was a pickup game at the park or shooting hoops in the driveway, he had that competitive spark but always with encouragement.

He was the kind of father who showed love through doing, showing up, providing, making sure you were cared for. He wasn't overly sentimental, but you never had to doubt where you stood with him. For me, I was always "Daddy's girl."

When I sat down to write his obituary, I wanted the world to know the man beyond the dates on paper. I wanted

them to see his laughter, his spirit, his joy. I wrote a poem
that came straight from my heart:

Forever Daddy's Girl

You taught me strength without saying a word,
how to laugh loud and love even harder.
You showed me what it means to stand tall,
even when life tries to knock you down.
You were my first protector,
my first cheerleader,
my first example of what a man should be.
I'll carry your jokes in my pocket,
your lessons in my heart,
and your love in every breath I take.
Though you've left this world,
you haven't left me.
I'll always be your little girl,
and you'll always be my Daddy.

The days after his passing were a blur of responsibility. The
strong one doesn't have time to fall apart, she makes
arrangements, organizes details, keeps people fed, makes sure
the obituary is printed, and gets through the service without
collapsing.

THE COST OF RESILENCE

It's what I had always done. And in those days, I realized, this was resilience, yes, but it was also the cost of that resilience. The price of always being the one who could carry it.

I miss my father every single day. But his laughter, his generosity, his humor, they live in me. To carry them forward is the strongest thing I'll ever do.

When the funeral day came, I moved through it like I had rehearsed, greeting people, making sure things stayed on schedule, thanking guests for coming. I was still holding it together, still in organizer mode.

But when it was my turn to stand in front of the casket, everything slowed.

This would be the last time I would see my father.

The last time I could reach out, even if my hand would meet only stillness.

It was like my mind had been protecting me up until that second, holding the flood back, but now the dam broke. My knees felt weak. My chest tightened. And before I could catch my breath, I was in the middle of a full asthma attack. Someone rushed to get my inhaler. My hands were shaking, my vision blurring, my lungs fighting for air while my heart fought the truth.

THE DAY EVERYTHING SHATTERED

That was the moment it all hit me: I couldn't organize my way out of this. I couldn't be strong enough to undo it. My father was gone.

Segue to the Next Chapter

When the funeral was over and the last condolences had been offered, I thought I would finally have a chance to stop and feel it all. But there was no pause button. My mother's decline was impossible to ignore. She wasn't herself, not in the small ways that can be brushed off, but in the glaring, heartbreaking ways that changed everything. And once again, I had to push my grief aside, shift into caretaker mode, and figure out what to do next.

Reflection Prompts

- Who in your life has shaped your sense of humor or joy? How do you keep that alive in your life?
- When have you been *"the strong one"* in a moment of loss? What did it cost you?
- What's one small way you can honor a loved one you've lost in your daily life?

THE COST OF RESILENCE

- How do you balance honoring someone's memory with giving yourself permission to grieve?

Journal Prompts:

1. Write a letter to your loved one who has passed. What would you say if you had just one more moment with them?

2. Describe the hardest part of *"being the strong one"* during that season. What did you need in those moments that you didn't receive?

3. List three memories that capture the essence of your loved one, not their death, but their life. What do those moments teach you about love?

4. Write about the first time you allowed yourself to feel grief fully. What helped you get through it?

_____

_____

_____

_____

_____

_____

_____

_____

_____

_____

Nia M. Thomas
THE COST OF RESILENCE

_____

_____

_____

_____

_____

CHAPTER 10

Watching Her Fade

I started seeing subtle changes back in early 2024. They were small at first, the kind of things you could easily brush off if you wanted to. Mom forgot conversations we had just had, asked the same question twice in one hour, forgot names she had never stumbled over before, and needed a new car key cut every other month, as if her originals had vanished into thin air. It was strange.

I encouraged her to go to the doctor, and she told me she had appointments. But something about the way she said it never sat right. I started to think maybe she was lying to me, that she didn't want me to know the truth, or worse, that she didn't even realize she was making it up.

Then came October 2024. My phone rang: my dad was in the hospital. My sister and aunt were already there, handling things. I was in Texas, far away, feeling helpless. The next day was when everything shifted for me.

I called Mom to talk about insurance for Dad, making sure things were handled. Instead, she told me a story about cooking him breakfast that morning and him leaving early to go somewhere she wasn't sure about. My heart sank. Dad wasn't at work; he was lying in a hospital bed. When I hung up, I called my sister, and she told me the same thing: on the way to the hospital, Mom had to be reminded again that Dad was even there.

I was terrified. Within two hours, I booked a flight out of Texas and rushed to the airport. I wasn't prepared for what I walked into.

The house was a disaster, dishes stacked high, clothes scattered, and the smell of stale liquor and neglect heavy in the air. And my mom, she wasn't herself. She was disoriented, detached. I tried to get her to go see my dad, to face what was happening, but it was like pulling against a tide I couldn't stop. I cleaned, I begged, I tried to talk sense into her. That's when I realized Dad's drinking problem hadn't been his alone, it was theirs. I left New Jersey defeated. Nothing resolved. Nothing changed.

Over the next few months, calls from them became few and far between. When I called, they couldn't find their phones. Before leaving, I had set up an Alexa Echo so we could video chat and even bought a landline with labeled numbers for emergencies. Within two weeks, both were unplugged and missing. I felt helpless, forced to sit in Texas, praying and stressing every single day.

By March 2025, the cycle repeated. Another call: Dad was back in the hospital. This time, I wasn't as alarmed. I thought he would recover. But I was worried about Mom. I booked another flight. When I got there, I used her complaints of stomach pain as my chance to get her to the ER. I had to trick her, but it worked.

Sitting in the ER with her was like living inside a loop. For five hours, she cycled through the same questions, the same comments, the same motions. She was convincing, if you didn't know her, you might think she was fine. But I knew. And then came the story about my sister, the one who had been brain-dead for seven years. Mom told it as if they had just spoken, as if she was on her way over. I looked at the doctor and said, "Something is wrong."

That night, the doctor admitted her and pulled me aside. "You need rest," she told me. For the first time in a long time, I felt seen. Someone else finally understood.

But then came the mistake I regret: before leaving, a nurse asked if it would be okay to put Mom and Dad in the same room. I thought it would comfort them, calm them both down. I agreed. The next day, Mom was discharged, and Dad broke himself out of the hospital.

One month later, Dad was gone.

I had barely hugged him goodbye before leaving Jersey, a pit in my stomach telling me it might be the last time. I wasn't wrong.

When I returned for the funeral, grief wasn't something I could fully feel. Because how do you grieve one parent when the other is slipping away in front of you? Mom couldn't remember that Dad had passed. The morning of the service, she pulled me aside and asked, "Whose funeral are we going to?" My heart broke in two. Every reminder meant she was reliving the devastating news as if it were the first time, over and over again.

At the service, she was present but absent, withdrawn, disconnected. And in the weeks after, things spiraled further. Medicaid delays, waitlists, endless doctor appointments that felt like they led nowhere. Family tried to stay with her, but the burden was too heavy. Eventually, she was alone again.

Within weeks, the bottom fell out. The ambulance took her to the hospital, and within days, she was admitted into a behavioral facility for possible dementia.

WATCHING HER FADE

Two months passed before she was discharged. I flew back to Jersey to accept it, because she couldn't be safely discharged to live alone. For a month, I stayed with her. To my surprise, she did well. I set up cameras, arranged transportation, and for the first time in months, I felt a flicker of relief. She wanted to be at home, and I wanted to trust her. She managed her medication, ate better, and although she asked me for a beer twice, she seemed to be handling it.

But I knew I couldn't stay forever. I had to live my life, too. So, I set boundaries and returned to Texas.

Now, we talk daily. Her conversations sound more like the mom I remember. She still has moments of confusion, but it's not as bad as before. There's progress, even if it's fragile. Medicaid is still pending, appointments still pile up, and I still battle anxiety every day. Nightmares about her drinking, about something happening when I'm not there, still haunt me.

And the truth is, I am still struggling to find my way back from being her caregiver to being her daughter. Even now, love and duty blur together, and I don't always know how to separate them.

But there is hope. We are a work in progress. She is showing me resilience in her own way, and I am learning what it means to love someone in their most vulnerable state, while still protecting my own life and sanity. Watching her fade is still painful, but it doesn't feel like free fall anymore. It feels like a climb, steep, exhausting, but with glimpses of light along the way.

Reflection Prompts

- How do you cope when the person you love most starts to feel like a stranger?

- What does it mean to grieve someone who is still alive?

- How do you balance being a caregiver while still needing to be a son, daughter, spouse, or sibling?

- In what ways can you find small moments of hope, even during a slow decline?

Journal Prompts

1. Write about the moment you first realized something was changing in a loved one. How did it make you feel physically and emotionally?

2. What has been the hardest part of balancing being a caregiver and a child? Where do those roles clash for you?

3. Make a list of the small moments, however fleeting, when you've seen light, humor, or hope in the middle of decline. What do they remind you of?

4. Write a compassionate letter to yourself, releasing the guilt of not being able to "fix" everything. What truth do you need to hold onto when the weight feels too heavy?

_____

_____

_____

_____

_____

_____

_____

_____

Nia M. Thomas
THE COST OF RESILENCE

_____

_____

_____

_____

_____

CHAPTER 11

The Cost of Resilience: How I stopped calling pain strength

For most of my life, I wore resilience like a badge of honor. It was the word people used to describe me when they marveled at how I seemed to keep going, no matter what came my way. I told myself it was a compliment, proof that I was strong, unbreakable, even. But the truth was, my "resilience" was often just survival in disguise.

I knew how to function in chaos. I knew how to smile while hurting, to keep moving while bleeding, to make "fine" my default answer no matter how far from fine I actually was. I thought that was strength. I thought endurance was the same thing as healing. I didn't know that resilience, when left unchecked, could come at the cost of my own well-being.

In the span of just two years, I had four surgeries. The last of those surgeries was the hardest: a breast reduction, followed just three weeks later by a hysterectomy. The weeks of recovery that followed were brutal. My body ached, but the heavier pain was emotional and spiritual. I grieved not only the incisions and the swelling, but the loss of parts of myself that had always symbolized womanhood. Without a womb, I would never carry a child. Without the breasts I had lived with all my life, I felt stripped, unfamiliar, even boyish. I would look in the mirror and barely recognize the reflection staring back.

I wasn't just healing; I was mourning. Mourning the dream of motherhood. Mourning the body I once knew. Mourning the sense of femininity, I felt had been carved away piece by piece. Some days, I whispered to God, "What else can You take from me?" And yet, as the scars began to fade, I started to see them differently, not as shame, but as survival. My body had endured what my heart didn't think it could. I was still here. Scarred, yes. Changed forever, yes. But still here.

The heart palpitations came later, not after the surgeries, but during the decline of my parents' health. Stress, grief, and worry pressed so hard on my chest that my heart began to beat out of rhythm, skipping and racing until I thought it might stop altogether. I went through echocardiograms, stress tests, and weeks of heart monitoring before finally hearing what I already knew deep down: my heart wasn't failing, it was carrying too much. The

THE COST OF RESILENCE: HOW I STOPPED CALLING PAIN STRENGTH

palpitations weren't medical; they were emotional. They were anxiety and grief, trying to find a way out.

I had built a life on keeping it together, holding the weight, pushing through, proving that nothing could take me down. But there's a quiet danger in that. That's the hidden cost of resilience. When you're always the one who can handle it, people stop asking if you should have to. And sometimes, you stop asking yourself too.

During a women's wellness workshop, I was asked, "When did you realize your body was reacting to stress?"

I froze. My mind raced.

Was it when I was attacked growing up?

After I was raped?

Maybe it was after the split with my ex, or when my aunt passed away?

The truth is... stress had always been part of my life. I didn't recognize it as stress; I thought it was resilience. I believed that this, all of this, was just what it meant to be a "strong Black woman." You push through. You deal. You keep moving.

But the truth was that my body had been screaming at me for years, and I had learned to ignore it. It wasn't until the years between the breakup and before I met my husband that

Nia M. Thomas
THE COST OF RESILENCE

I started to break in ways I couldn't hide: panic attacks, sleepless nights, numbness, crying for no reason and not being able to stop. Depression and anxiety started to show up as if they had always lived in my body. That's when I knew something had to change. I could no longer fake it or wear "strength" like armor. My body wasn't letting me.

When I first realized my body was breaking down under the weight of everything I'd carried, trauma, loss, performance, and pressure, I did what I thought I was supposed to do: I found a therapist.

But it wasn't the experience I hoped for.

She didn't look like me.

She didn't sound like me.

She didn't come from where I came from.

Instead of a safe space, therapy felt like a battleground.

I was defending who I was more than I was discovering who I could be.

I kept showing up, hoping it would shift. But it didn't.

Eventually, I moved to Texas and started life over again.

I figured I'd left all that stress behind, but I hadn't, because it was still inside me.

THE COST OF RESILENCE: HOW I STOPPED CALLING PAIN STRENGTH

When the pandemic hit and the world stood still, everything I had tucked away came rushing back, grief, fear, anxiety. It felt like I couldn't keep up with my own thoughts.

So, I went back to that same therapist.

A few sessions in, she ghosted me.

No explanation.

Just... gone.

And I told myself, "Maybe therapy isn't for me."

But deep down, I knew I still needed help.

Still needed healing.

The pain didn't go away. I couldn't pray it away, overwork it away, or numb it away. I knew I had to try again.

I searched inconsistently over the next few years, but I never gave up. This time, I was determined to find someone who looked like me, someone who could hold my story without judgment or confusion.

Then, about a month before my father passed, something shifted.

I was on a plane ride home and, once again, decided to try because things were getting rough.

Same search tools. Same directories. But this time... something clicked.

It felt like divine intervention.

THE COST OF RESILENCE

I found her.

A Black woman therapist. Someone who got it.

I booked my first appointment before the plane even landed.

I didn't know then how much I would need her in the weeks to come. But God did.

That's when the real work began.

It was one of the best decisions I've ever made.

With her, I started unpacking years of unspoken trauma. I began to understand how I had lived without boundaries. I said "yes" when I had nothing left to give. I answered calls at all hours, worked sixty-plus hour weeks, skipped breaks, ignored meals, and poured myself into everyone except me.

That started to change.

I began choosing me. And at first, that felt selfish, but it was necessary.

I thought I had done the "strong woman" thing right.

But therapy showed me where I had been bleeding emotionally and calling it "resilience."

It showed me how long I'd lived without boundaries.

How many times I had said yes when I had nothing left to give.

THE COST OF RESILENCE: HOW I STOPPED CALLING PAIN STRENGTH

How often I had answered the phone at 1:00 a.m. because someone else needed me more than I needed rest.

How I had worked sixty-plus hours a week and called it purpose.

Therapy helped me realize that I didn't just need rest, I deserved it.

That rest is resistance.

That saying no doesn't make me selfish.

It makes me whole.

I started caring for myself in ways I didn't think I had time for.

Now, I set boundaries, not out of bitterness, but out of love. I still mean well, but I love me, too. No more working past exhaustion. No more sacrificing my peace for people who would never do the same. I use the word "no" with love and intention. I've learned that rest is a right, not a reward.

I started caring for myself in small, intentional ways. Sometimes that looked like a nap. Other times it was a walk, a long shower, or a full day at the spa. I took myself out to dinner. I got back into the gym, where I always felt most like myself. Walking became therapy. Writing returned. Joy followed.

This is what wellness looks like for me.

THE COST OF RESILENCE

Not just bubble baths and affirmations, but boundaries.

Not just quiet time, but knowing I deserve peace, daily.

This didn't happen overnight. I'm still on the journey. But it's the best journey I've ever been on.

As I worked through therapy, I began to see patterns that had been forming for decades. They didn't start in my adult life, they had been with me since childhood.

Flashback: The Early Signs

Looking back, maybe it all started much earlier than I realized.

From a young age, I carried a sense of responsibility that didn't feel optional, it just felt like part of who I was. Around seven or eight years old, I would host bake sales and somehow get my hands on baby clothes to sell. I couldn't tell you where those clothes came from, but I'd always find a way to turn them into something someone might buy.

By eighth grade, I found out my dad had been laid off. There were no visible changes in our household, our lifestyle remained the same, and my needs and wants were still met, but I immediately decided to get a job. It was as if some switch inside me flipped, telling me, *You have to step up now.*

THE COST OF RESILENCE: HOW I STOPPED CALLING PAIN STRENGTH

No one told me I had to do this, and I never felt pressured, it was simply how I operated.

In high school, that instinct only grew. At one point, I was juggling three jobs while going to school full-time. I had this little hustle in me, this mindset that I needed to take care of things, to figure things out. It was just... me.

Social things like prom felt almost frivolous. Somewhere deep down, I believed my time and energy should be focused on responsibility, not celebration. I told myself I was being mature, but in reality, I was quietly trading pieces of my youth for the weight I thought I needed to carry. And so, I did.

Looking back, it's no wonder I wore my strength like armor. Those early choices, though made with good intentions, taught me that worth was earned through responsibility, not rest. And that belief followed me well into adulthood, shaping how I carried pain and called it strength.

Closing Reflection

I didn't realize it then, but those early choices were shaping how I handled pain and pressure as an adult. I was so used to jumping into action, so used to carrying the load, that I never

THE COST OF RESILENCE

considered if I was actually okay. I didn't know the difference between being capable and being consumed.

It took years, and more than a few moments of breaking down behind closed doors, for me to understand that resilience without rest, without vulnerability, without space to feel, is not resilience at all. It's a slow kind of self-erasure.

Now, when people call me strong, I no longer hear it as a requirement to perform. I've learned that true resilience doesn't mean never falling apart, it means giving yourself permission to fall apart and still believing you're worthy in the process.

These patterns didn't break overnight. But every boundary I now set, every time I say "no" or choose rest, I'm healing that younger version of me, the little girl who thought strength meant never asking for help.

I used to think survival was the goal, pushing through, staying strong, keeping it all together. But now I know healing is the goal: choosing me, over and over again. Resting without guilt. Saying no without apology. Loving myself not just when it's convenient, but when it's critical. And for the first time in my life, I'm not just surviving, I'm living.

Now, I know better.

THE COST OF RESILENCE: HOW I STOPPED CALLING PAIN STRENGTH

Resilience isn't about enduring everything. It's about honoring yourself enough to say, *I deserve peace, too.*

Reflection Prompts

- Have you ever felt like therapy wasn't made for someone like you? How did that shape your healing journey?

- In what ways have you ignored your body's signals that you were overwhelmed or burned out?

- What would it look like to treat rest not as a reward but as a right?

- Where in your life are you still saying yes when your soul is screaming no?

- How can you redefine what "strength" means for you?

Journal Prompt

Write about the younger version of you who thought she had to be strong all the time. What do you want her to know now about rest, boundaries, and healing?

_____

_____

_____

_____

_____

_____

_____

CHAPTER 12

What Resilience Really Looks Like

One morning, I sat in my living room in Texas, tea in hand, staring out the window at nothing in particular. The house was quiet, but my mind wasn't quiet.

I thought about everything.

About my father, gone.

About my mom, slipping further away.

About my husband, still locked up.

About all the surgeries, the moves, the funerals, the phone calls that broke me, and the ones that held me together.

And I thought about the fact that I was still here.

People call me "strong" all the time, like it's a compliment. They say it with admiration, with respect, with awe. And I nod. I say, "Thank you."

But here's the truth about resilience: it's not glamorous.

It's not the Instagram quotes. It's not the "strong Black woman" archetype people love to glorify.

Real resilience is messy.

THE COST OF RESILENCE

It's crying on your lunch break and then logging back in to run a meeting.

It's wiping your tears in the bathroom at your niece's school before meeting her teacher.

It's holding the phone to your ear for prison calls and smiling so he can hear hope in your voice, even when you don't feel any.

It's waking up with swollen eyes from crying the night before and still showing up for work; Zoom enhancements hiding the evidence but not the exhaustion.

It's making dinner while your mind is replaying hospital conversations you wish you could forget.

It's going for a run, not because you feel motivated, but because you're trying to outrun the heaviness for just thirty minutes.

It's taking a deep breath in the grocery store aisle because you almost broke down between the cereal and the canned beans.

It's answering the phone when you don't want to talk because someone on the other end needs you more than you need the silence.

It's sitting across from your mom in the weeks after your dad's death, listening to her confusedly talk as if he'd just walked to the store, and having to gently, patiently remind her he was gone, even when your own grief was fresh and raw. It's holding those conversations together with tears secretly falling because you had no real time to grieve.

It's sitting with a funeral director, holding a pen you can barely grip because your hands are trembling, signing papers you wish you never had to sign.

It's standing in a florist shop, picking out flowers for your father's casket, holding back tears while strangers ask if you need help finding something.

It's the fight you had with yourself to get out of bed, and the quiet victory when you did.

It's leaving a meeting, crying for five minutes, and then splashing water on your face so you can go to your next meeting like nothing happened.

It's the moments when your hands are shaking, but you keep dialing the number.

It's the apology you give when you snap at someone you love because stress spilled out sideways, and the grace you try to give yourself for being human.

Resilience is all of that.

THE COST OF RESILENCE

It's ugly crying, deep sighs, broken prayers, and whispered promises to yourself that you'll try again tomorrow.

Rest is Resistance

Somewhere along this journey, my therapist said something that changed everything:

"Rest is resistance."

At first, I didn't fully understand it.

Because I was raised to believe rest was for after the work was done.

But when is the work ever done?

For women, especially for Black women, there is always something more to carry. Another person to care for, another crisis to manage, another room to perform in. Rest starts to feel like a luxury instead of a right.

I learned that rest isn't quitting.

It isn't weakness.

It's resistance against a world that tells us our worth is only in what we produce, repair, give, or sacrifice.

There were days when resilience looked like powering through, but there were also days when resilience looked like closing my laptop, turning off my phone, and taking a nap.

WHAT RESILENCE REALLY LOOKS LIKE

I want other women to know: you do not have to burn yourself down to prove you're strong. Sometimes the bravest thing you can do is stop.

Lessons From the Cracks

Looking back, I can see how every broken moment shaped me, not into a flawless picture of strength, but into a living, breathing human example of resilience.

I learned that resilience is not about being unshaken. It's about being willing to rise again, even with the cracks showing.

I learned that asking for help is not failure, it's wisdom.

I learned that leadership, love, and caregiving don't require you to disappear in the process.

And I learned that resilience has to include joy. Because without joy, you're not really surviving, you're just enduring.

Closing Reflection

When I think about resilience now, I don't see a superhero cape.

I see all the mornings I got out of bed when I didn't want to.

I see the therapy sessions where words finally spilled out of me after years of silence.

THE COST OF RESILENCE

I see the walks at lunch; the moments I used movement as medicine.

I see the deep breaths before hard conversations, the ones that made my chest tight but left me stronger after speaking my truth.

I see the way I've learned to cry, to rest, and still show up.

For so long, I thought resilience meant never breaking. Never crying. Never letting anyone see me stumble. But now I know, true resilience isn't about holding everything together, it's about having the courage to fall apart while still believing in your ability to rise again.

Resilience looks like scars. It looks like surgeries and grief, and still choosing to move forward anyway. It looks like carrying children who aren't your own and loving them fiercely as if they were. It looks like burying parents and still showing up at work the next morning because you didn't know how else to survive.

Resilience is messy. It's cracked voices on phone calls. It's swollen eyes on Zoom meetings. Its broken prayers whispered at midnight, when you're not even sure God is listening, but you pray anyway.

WHAT RESILENCE REALLY LOOKS LIKE

But resilience is also soft. It's choosing rest when the world says keep pushing. It's redefining strength so it includes naps, boundaries, and saying no. It's allowing yourself to feel joy again without guilt. It's learning that being strong and being soft are not opposites they are both survivals.

When I look back now, I realize that resilience has always been in the small things, not the grand ones. It's in the meals I still cooked, the laughter I still managed to find, the way I picked up the phone one more time when I wanted to throw it across the room. It's in every choice to stay, to love, to heal.

And maybe that's the biggest thing I've learned, resilience isn't about what you push through.

It's about what you allow yourself to soften into.

It's about showing up cracked but still whole, scarred but still beautiful, tired but still willing.

So, when people call me strong now, I don't hear it as a command to keep carrying everything. I hear it as a reminder: I am still here. And that is enough.

And for you, the one holding this book in your hands, if you've ever wondered if you could survive the weight of your story, let my life be your proof. You already have. You are already resilient.

Reflection Prompt

Think about the moments in your life when you thought you wouldn't make it through, but you did.

- What got you through those moments?
- Were you powering through, or did you find moments to pause and rest?
- How can you give yourself permission to rest more, even when life feels demanding?

WHAT RESILENCE REALLY LOOKS LIKE

Journal Prompt

Write a letter to yourself as if you are your own healer.

- Remind yourself of what you've survived.

- Tell yourself where you've been too hard on yourself.

- Tell her that resilience can look like naps, saying no, asking for help, and choosing joy.

_____

_____

_____

_____

_____

_____

_____

_____

_____

_____

_____

_____

_____

_____

_____

_____

EPILOGUE

The Journey Continues

It's been a long road, hasn't it? From grief to growth, from loss to love, and all the messy middle in between. As I write this today, I'm still learning what resilience means every single day. Writing this book has been a powerful part of my healing journey, putting my pain and my progress onto paper has helped me make sense of the chaos, find meaning in the struggle, and honor how far I've come.

I've come a long way, but I still have room to continue healing and growing. Life keeps moving, challenges keep coming, and resilience isn't a finish line, it's a daily practice. This book isn't the end of my story; it's just one chapter in an ongoing journey. And I hope it has been a companion for yours.

THE COST OF RESILENCE

"You may be knocked down many times, but you are never required to stay there." — *Nia M. Thomas*

"Do not search for healing in the hands that caused your wounds. Your wholeness is waiting where love and truth live." — *Nia M. Thomas*

A Final Hug

Dear Sister in Strength,

You've reached the end of this book, but not the end of your story.

If you've read these pages, you've walked with me through heartbreak, resilience, love, loss, and healing. And maybe you saw pieces of yourself here, the grief you didn't say out loud, the strength you didn't think anyone noticed, the moments when you thought you couldn't take one more step.

When you opened this book, maybe you were carrying more than your share too. Maybe you were the one everyone calls when things fall apart. Maybe you were "the strong one" for so long, you don't even remember what it feels like to set that weight down.

I didn't write this book because I have all the answers. I wrote it because I know the questions that keep us up at night. The "how am I supposed to keep going?" questions. The "why me?" questions. The "will I ever feel like myself again?" questions.

THE COST OF RESILENCE

This wasn't a story about perfection, it's a story about survival, grace, and resilience. Some pages were heavy. Some were soft. All of them were honest.

Here's what I need you to hear before you close this book:

You are not broken beyond repair.

You are not invisible.

You are not "just strong", you are allowed to be soft too.

Life will keep happening. There will be moments you think you can't keep standing. But you can. You will. And you don't have to do it alone.

I don't have all the answers. But I do have proof, living, breathing proof, that we can survive things that once felt unsurvivable. That we can lose and still love again. That we can crack and still rise.

My hope is that as you read, you not only saw my story, but you saw your own. And maybe, just maybe, you realize you've been stronger than you thought all along.

So if you take nothing else from these pages, take this: you are still here, and that is enough.

With love and resilience,

Nia

Acknowledgments

First and foremost, I give thanks to God, for carrying me through seasons I thought would destroy me, and for reminding me that even in the darkest places, light can still break through.

Special thanks to my husband, who kept giving me the push and strength I needed to get through the writing process. You are my heart. Your love, encouragement, and resilience kept me grounded when life was anything but steady. When I was doubtful, fearful, and downright consumed with worry, you were there for me. I couldn't have written this book without you.

To my cousin, who read and listened tirelessly through draft after draft and cheered me on, thank you for being my sounding board.

To my therapist, who not only helped me process pain but also gave me the courage and push to write this story, thank you for guiding me toward healing and helping me see the power in putting my truth on paper.

And finally, to you, the reader holding this book, thank you. This is not just my story; it is ours. If even one piece of these pages brings you healing, hope, or courage, then it was worth writing.

About The Author

Nia M. Thomas is a storyteller, leader, and advocate for resilience. A successful corporate professional and mentor, she has guided leaders, built teams, and broken barriers as a Black woman in corporate America. Beyond her professional achievements, she has faced profound personal challenges, grief, caregiving, health struggles, and the weight of starting over, and turned them into lessons of strength and hope.

Her writing blends raw honesty with reflection, inviting readers to confront their own pain while finding the courage to heal. When she's not writing, she pours into her community, mentors emerging leaders, and continues her own journey of growth and wellness.

Nia writes under her pen name to honor both her private journey and the universal nature of resilience, reminding readers that behind every polished surface is a story worth telling.

Connect with Nia

◆ **X (Twitter):** @BehindThePenNia

◆ **Instagram:** @behindthepennia

◆ **TikTok:** @NiaMThomas

◆ **Linktree:** linktr.ee/behindthepennia